WOMEN Wonderfully MADE

MOTHER'S BOOK

written by
ALICIA HERNON

the
messy family
project®

Dear Mom,

We are so happy you have purchased this book because it is our desire that this tool begin a new and deeper relationship between you and your daughter. She needs you as a guide for the transitions she is going through now, in the coming months, and even in the years ahead.

If you have not purchased the Daughter's Book, you must do so to reap the full benefit of this course! The Daughter's book is a workbook for your daughter to interview you, process information, and record the ways in which she is going to apply the information that will be presented. It is essential!

While these books can be used by themselves, we wanted to let you know that there are more resources available to you. You can scan the code here to check them out!

At the link, you will find a printable My Personal Proverbs chart referenced in the book, coloring pages for your daughter, and some sample clips of our course videos.

Our course videos are designed to accompany this book. Some moms are comfortable presenting information about adolescence in their own words, and if that describes you, great! We are happy that you have this workbook to help you. But if you'd rather not have the pressure, I can present the information so you can sit with your daughter, follow along with the book, and answer her questions, then check out our videos!

Either way, welcome to Women Wonderfully Made, and we hope you are enriched by what you discover in this teaching guide and companion daughter's workbook. By the end, we hope that both of you are inspired to give thanks to our Heavenly Father Who made every woman perfectly and wonderfully.

In Him,

Alicia and the Messy Family Project team

Preparing for the course

As you know, women are in a battle in our culture today. The same culture that seeks to redefine human life and marriage also seeks to re-define what it means to be a woman. We've found this course to be a helpful tool to enable our daughters to understand their womanhood and the feminine vocation.

A bit of history: this course is inspired by one designed by a Christian homeschooling mother, Doran Richards. She was not only pro-life but anti-contraception as well. I loved this course so much I went through it with four of my six daughters. For several years I taught her course to others. However, I felt that it needed a fuller Catholic perspective, using the writings of the saints, St. John Paul II's Theology of the Body, and the example of Our Lady. The result is what you are reading now.

My goal is to empower YOU as the mother to mentor your daughter. Please understand this! **Although this course is meant to help you, it can never replace you.** My goal is to set you up as a trusted guide for your daughter - a safe person who she can confide in, recieve information from, and ask questions to. This book is to help you begin these conversations with her.

Before taking this course, **prepare a space that is private** where the two of you can talk without being overheard and you can both share things that are private and delicate. Respect her natural modesty, and let her know you are available to speak with her again whenever she needs to .

As a mom of many daughters, I completely understand if it is difficult to connect with your daughter at this juncture in her life. I found in doing this course that it was easier to talk to some of my daughters than others. For a time this bothered me, but then I came to realize that sometimes we just have different temperaments and approaches from our daughters, and that while that can be frustrating, it is also a reflection that God made each of us uniquely, and this is part of His plan. As mothers, we might just have to work harder to connect with some of our children than others, and that's ok.

What is important is that as much as you and your daughter might differ, that through this course, she comes to understand that **she is special to you, that you accept her as a gift from God, and that you love her and want to seek to understand her**. Also you want her to understand that what she is going through is something that other girls and other women can also understand and empathize with!

WHEN TO DO THIS COURSE

Ideally, you should give this course to your daughter before she begins puberty so that she can have a heads up about what is going on. As you may know, sometimes the hormonal changes of puberty can make a parent feel like their little girl has become a quarrelsome stranger, so it's easier to do this course before that all begins.

But if your daughter is already in the throes of puberty, it's not too late! This information and guidance is super-helpful even for older girls.

FYI In this course, we will NOT be giving "The Talk"; aka: we will not be discussing the sexual act or where babies come from. That's a talk for another time, one that our family usually reserves for a weekend retreat that we call the "Growing Up Weekend." During this course, we will be talking only about the female body, not the male body. However, this course might lead to curiosity and questions, so let your daughter know that she can ask you anything. A good guide when answering her questions is to give her less information, not more. If she wants more information, she will ask for it. Girls mature at different times and it is important that she is given sensitive information only when she is mature enough to receive it.

SETTING THE STAGE

First of all, make sure your daughter has a blank version of the **Daughter's Workbook** to use with this course. If you don't have one, you can get one from MessyFamilyProject.org. The daughter workbook has graphics, fill in the blanks and coloring pages. We've also included white space on the Scripture pages for her to doodle, draw, or copy down and decorate a verse from the Bible that speaks to them. She can keep it as a reference when the course it over. So make sure your daughter has a copy of this wonderful resource!

Throughout the course, your daughter will be filling in answers in **her workbook**. She can do this during the talk, or she can do it afterwards. You decide what is best for her. For some girls writing while listening helps, but for others it can be a huge distraction. There is no one "right" way to use the Girl's workbook! The Mom's workbook has the answers for all the questions, but she will also hear them in the presentations.

You may want to use some of the pages in the workbook to create a small scrapbook. If you intend to do the Growing Up Weekend with her later, the scrapbook pages she creates can be incorporated into the book for that course. That is entirely up to you.

Also, she should have **a Bible**. Every girl this age should have her own Bible, so make her a gift of one! During the course, we will be giving out Scriptures for the girls to copy down. Copying down Scripture is a sacramental: an instrument of grace. It's important for girls to know how to look up Scripture and transcribe it themselves.

We'll also be sharing a volume of the Book of Proverbs and a calendar for understanding her cycle. She also needs a set of markers or pencils including the colors green, yellow, pink, and red for coloring.

Again, the purpose of this course is to begin a conversation with your daughter that will extend after the course is over. The workbooks are to help your daughter internalize the information learned so she can return to it and you can refer to it to help her understand herself. The mother's workbook contains the same material as the girl's book (you'll notice we are addressing your daughter in the text) but with additional supplemental information, including answers to some of the various quizzes.

Thanks again for taking this course and know that I and my team will be praying for you and your daughter as you doW! After this page, the rest of the book is directed to your daughter. **You may want to start with the Introduction "Why are we doing this course?"** before getting into the first session. If you purchase the videos, you can just follow along with your book as I present the information to her.

Let's get started.

Why are we doing this course?

To be ready for the changes coming

One of the biggest changes you will go through in your life is the transition from girlhood to womanhood. For some girls, this time can be full of questions, worry, or even fear, but the way to conquer these feelings is through gaining wisdom by understanding. Wisdom and understanding can help us avoid unnecessary suffering and carry the suffering we can't escape with dignity and even joy. There is nothing that we can't handle with God's help!

Knowing about your body, learning what is normal and what is not, and growing in your relationship with your mom and other women will help this transition be a time of growth not just physically, but spiritually and emotionally as well.

We want you to connect with your own mom in understanding this plan, and with other girls and women so you can learn and seek wisdom together. Understanding our bodies and ourselves, enables us to more deeply appreciate our calling as women.

To take responsibility for our bodies

When you were a baby, your mom and dad did everything for you! They fed you, dressed you, and changed your diaper. But now, you do all those things for yourself (except for the diaper part, I hope!). As you grew, you took more and more responsibility for yourself. In this course, we are going to talk about how you can support your body in the big changes that are coming. This is important because you will need to take care of your body your whole life! This is part of growing up.

Why is your feminine body so important? Because you, along with every woman, were created to bear life within you! **This is our superpower!**

Because our bodies have the amazing ability to nurture life, we need to be very aware of how we use our body, how we feed our body, and how we care for our body. A woman's body is complex and intricately designed, and it needs to be cared for very intentionally. At times, problems that women experience with their bodies have to do with the lack of care that they give it. In this course we will talk about how you can start now to take responsibility for the beautiful body God has given you.

> "The moral and spiritual strength of a woman is joined to her awareness that God entrusts the human being to her in a special way."
>
> **ON THE DIGNITY AND VOCATION OF WOMEN**

To praise God that you are wonderfully made

God made you a woman. It was His choice. Up until now, it might have seemed a little random—why are you a girl and not a boy? The simple answer is that God chose to create you as a girl. He gave you a female body, and as you grow, He will begin to show you the wonderful and exciting plan He has for you as a woman.

Being a woman doesn't mean wearing pink or liking sparkling things. It doesn't mean wearing skirts or high heels. Being a woman means we are honored by God to have the capacity to bring forth life. Men have not been given this gift! Each of us was born inside another woman: our mothers! Being a woman means being part of the human race that brings the rest of us into existence. This is not something we should resent or hate or fear. It's something that we should praise God for.

God designed our bodies with particular care. We are His crown of creation—the last thing God created, according to the Bible, was woman, and it's clear we are meant to be His masterpiece. Following the example of Mary, our Blessed Mother, we can learn to fully embrace how we have been made by our perfect Heavenly Father and join with her in praising God for being "fearfully and wonderfully made"!

My soul proclaims the greatness of the LORD;

my spirit rejoices in GOD MY SAVIOR!

LUKE 1:46-47

Wonderfully Made - Our Body's Design

We all have a body—there are bodies everywhere we look! So in some ways, bodies are very ordinary. But we are called by God to see ourselves and others differently. We are all actually quite extraordinary! **Women especially have a design that reveals the presence of a Creator**, a loving and infinitely wise Father, who has a plan for each of us. And His design is amazing!

> "'The revelation of the body' helps us in some way to discover the extraordinary nature of what is ordinary."
>
> **ST. JOHN PAUL II**

Basic Body Design

You probably know what your body looks like from the outside: now we will be discussing what it looks like from the inside.

The Female Body - Side View

We are clearly wonderfully and compactly made! This illustration of the female body contains elements from different systems: digestive, excretory, and even skeletal—but it shows how the reproductive system of women is nestled among them. We're using this view so you can see where your reproductive organs are in relation to the parts you are already familiar with, such as the pubic bone or the bladder.

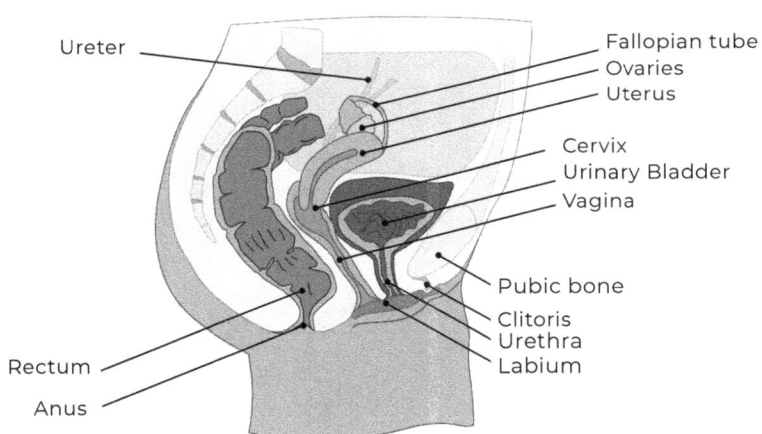

GLOSSARY OF TERMS:

- **Ureter:** The tube connecting the kidneys to the bladder

- **Fallopian tube:** Two slender ducts that connect the ovaries to the uterus. An egg travels from the ovaries to the uterus through these tubes during ovulation.

- **Ovaries:** The female reproductive gland in which ova—eggs—are produced.

- **Uterus:** Also known as the womb!

- **Cervix:** A neck-like structure at the outer end of the uterus.

- **Urinary Bladder:** The sac that stores urine before it's released

- **Vagina:** the opening which leads to the uterus

- **Pubic bone:** This bone cradles your organs and is connected to your thigh bones.

- **Clitoris:** a small sensitive organ located at the top of the vulva

- **Urethra:** The opening that allows liquid waste to exit the body

- **Labium:** The outer and inner lips protecting the vagina

- **Rectum:** A tube where solid waste is stored before it passes out of the anus

- **Anus:** the opening that allows solid waste to pass out of the body

The Female Body - Bottom View

THE FEMALE BODY CONTAINS THREE OPENINGS

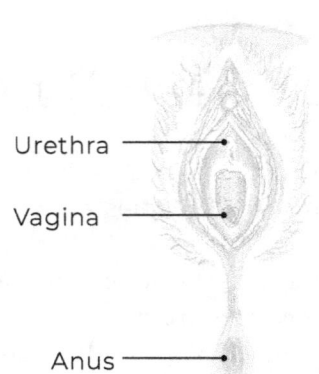

- **Urethra**: the opening that allows liquid waste to pass out of the body
- **Vagina**: the opening which leads to the uterus. It's also known as the birth canal and is protected by two layers of labia. The menstrual flow exits the body through this opening.
- **Anus**: the opening that allows solid waste to pass out of the body

The Female Reproductive System - Front View

Now let's look at the reproductive system of a woman's body. This diagram has expanded definitions from the one above.

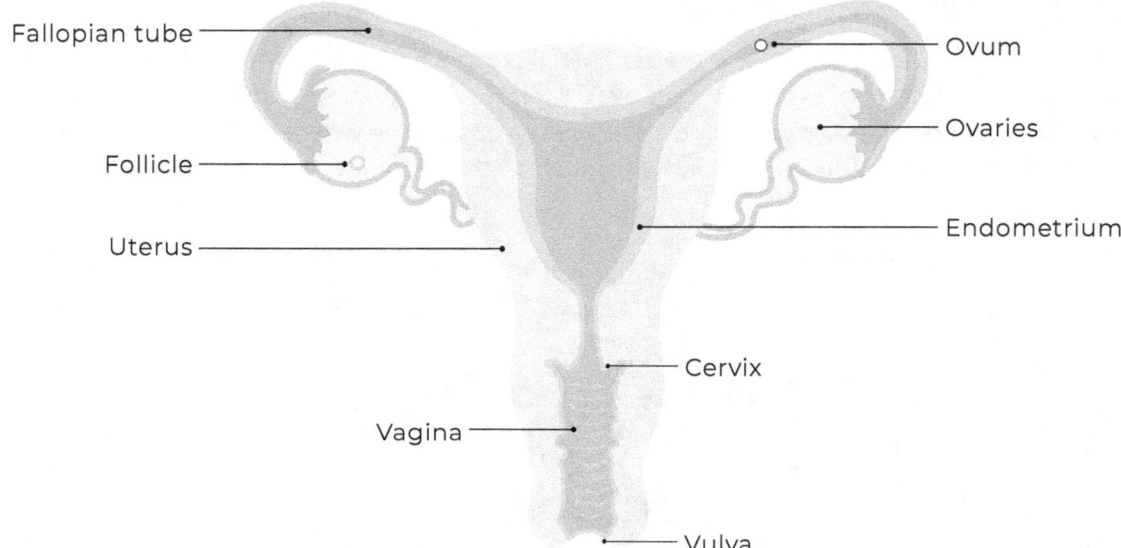

GLOSSARY OF TERMS:

- **Ovaries:** The female reproductive gland in which ova—"eggs"—are produced. Each woman has two ovaries which release eggs in turn, so that each ovary can rest for a month before releasing another.

- **Ovum:** The female reproductive cells found in the ovaries in the female body. Ovum is the Latin word for egg, and the plural is ova.

- **Follicles:** From a Latin word that means "little sacks." In the ovaries, each egg is nested inside its own follicle, or egg sac.

- **Fallopian tubes:** Two slender ducts that connect the ovaries to the uterus. An egg travels from the ovaries to the uterus through these tubes during ovulation.

- **Uterus or Womb:** A hollow, muscular organ, where babies are nourished prior to birth. It's normally hard and smooth, but it develops a soft lining during the cycle that can nurture a baby during pregnancy.

- **Endometrium:** A mucous membrane that lines the uterus. It thickens and is shed during a monthly cycle.

- **Cervix:** A neck-like structure at the outer end of the uterus.

- **Vagina or Birth canal:** The passage leading from the uterus to the vulva.

- **Vulva:** The external parts of the female genitalia. This is the outside opening to the vagina which can be seen.

What is a Cycle?

God designed the world to experience seasons of growth, blooming, dying off, and resting. We call these yearly seasons spring, summer, autumn, and winter. Did you know that women's bodies have seasons as well? When a girl becomes a woman, her cycle happens every month for about thirty to forty years. During that time, most women marry and have children. This cycle prepares and enables women to have children and cleanses her body on a regular basis to keep her healthy.

When a baby girl is formed in her mother's womb, God gives her a set of about a million eggs which are stored in two sacs. When a girl becomes a woman, these eggs begin to be released from their sacs. The microscopic eggs are released one at a time every <u>month</u>. The process that a woman's body goes through—releasing this egg, moving it through her body and breaking it down—is called the <u>menstrual cycle</u>.

Here are the <u>four</u> seasons of the menstrual cycle. Just as seeds grow in the ground for a long time before people realize that spring has come, so the first stage, the follicular stage, happens without our being aware of it at first.

 **FOLLICULAR PHASE**

How long does it last?

<u>3-5</u> days

What happens during this stage?

<u>GROWING</u>. During this stage, one <u>ovary</u> is preparing to release an egg. Scientists call it the follicular stage because the follicle or egg sac that is releasing an <u>egg</u> swells during this stage.

Is it visible or invisible?

Mostly <u>invisible</u>. What happens here is mostly invisible and undetectable. Think of it as spring, when seeds are swelling and sprouting silently and moving upwards to the sun before anyone notices.

What is happening in the uterus?

Inside you, the lining of the uterus begins to <u>soften</u> and <u>thicken</u>.

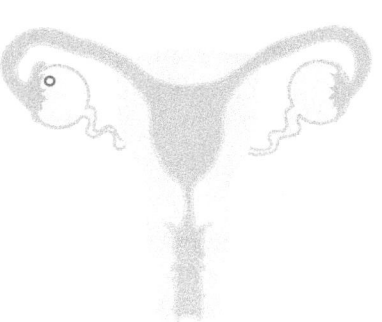

Summer
OVULATION

How long does it last?

<u>5-7</u> days

What happens during this stage?

<u>BLOOMING</u>. In this stage, the <u>egg</u> actually is released from its sac and travels through the <u>fallopian tube</u> to the <u>uterus</u>. This is called ovulation.

Is it visible or invisible?

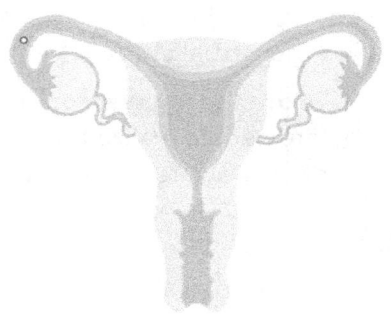

Mostly <u>invisible</u>. Some women notice a bit of clear <u>discharge</u> coming from their cervix. This discharge looks like a kind of stretchy mucus at the beginning but gradually becomes thicker and drier towards the end.

What is happening in the uterus?

The lining of the <u>uterus</u> continues to <u>thicken</u>. Once the egg is released, it will remain in the uterus for about a day before dissolving within your body.

Autumn
LUTEAL PHASE

How long is this stage?

<u>12-14</u> days

What happens during this stage?

<u>FALLING</u>. The <u>egg</u> within the uterus disintegrates and the <u>lining</u> of the <u>uterus</u> prepares to be shed. We can think of this stage as autumn, when flowers lose their petals, leaves change color from green to golden or red or brown.

Is it invisible or visible?

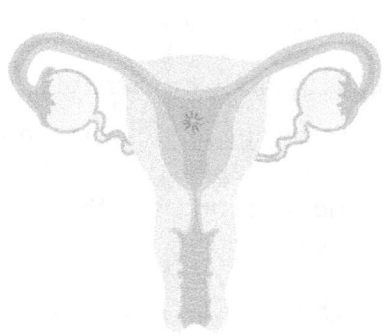

Mostly <u>invisible</u>. Most women have little to no <u>discharge</u>. At the end of the stage, some women experience premenstrual syndrome, or <u>PMS</u>, as the body prepares for menstruation. This can include slight cramping, breast tenderness, and food cravings.

What is happening in the uterus?

At the beginning of this phase, the discharge from the ovulation stage changes from clear to <u>yellow</u>, which is why it's known as "luteal" (yellow). At the end of this phase the <u>endometrium</u> begins to fall off in pieces.

Winter MENSTRUATION

How long does it last?

<u>3-5</u> days

What happens during this stage?

<u>CLEANSING</u>. The difference between cleaning and cleansing is that cleansing uses liquid. Think of it as your personal winter season, where the special preparation for the egg and the <u>endometrium</u> is washed out of your body, just as snow and rain wash the earth.

Is it visible or invisible?

<u>Visible</u>. This is the most <u>visible</u> stage of your cycle. Because this end of the cycle is so obvious, some women refer to it as a 'period,' just like a period ends a sentence. But it's important to recognize that menstruation isn't your entire cycle or even most of your cycle: it's the <u>ending</u> of a process of four seasons of a full cycle of growth, blooming, falling, and cleansing.

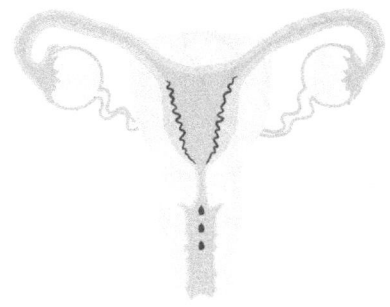

What is happening in the uterus?

It makes sense that all the special preparation for the egg and the lining of the uterus would need to be washed out of our bodies. So God designed menstruation. The liquid He uses to wash away the egg and the lining and cleanse our insides is blood. During menstruation, the soft lining of the uterus (the <u>endometrium</u>) breaks off and flows out through your <u>vagina</u> for about three to five days. The length of your flow can vary and may not be regular when you first begin your period or for the first year of your cycle. It's usually not very heavy, about a tablespoon of blood a day, about <u>1-5</u> tablespoons overall.

So God created mankind in His own image,
in the image of God He created them;
male and female He created them.

...God saw all that He had made, and it was very good.

GEN 1:27

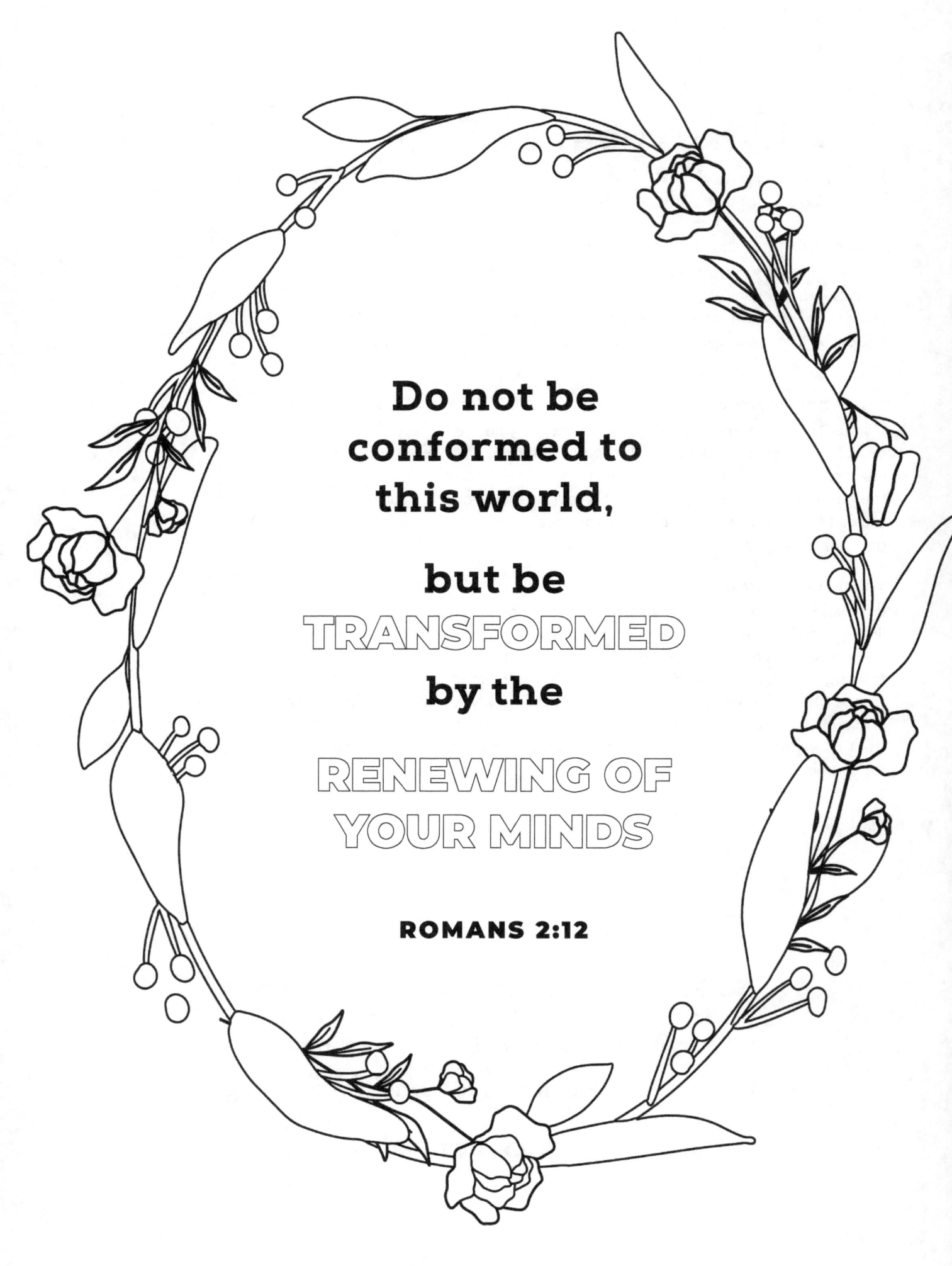

Do not be conformed to this world,

but be
TRANSFORMED
by the

RENEWING OF
YOUR MINDS

ROMANS 2:12

Renewing our Minds

According to the world, a woman's cycle is seen as <u>an inconvenience</u>, <u>a "curse,"</u> <u>something to be ignored or suffered through</u>. Some areas of medicine actually try to control women's bodies, through the use of chemical hormones which actually can stop a woman's natural cycle instead of supporting it.

But it would be wrong and irreverent of us to ignore how our Father God designed us. We need to be transformed in our understanding of women's bodies through the renewal of our mind.

Women need to learn to <u>listen</u> to their bodies. When our body says "rest," we need to learn to rest. When our body says "Go!" we need to learn to go. Perhaps the world wants women to be just like men? Men don't have cycles, but we are not men. Our bodies are not the same, nor should they be.

In the Old Testament, when a woman had discharge she was seen as being "unclean," so when she had her period or after having a baby she was isolated, put in a tent where no men were allowed and waited on hand and foot by other women. Honestly, that doesn't sound too bad! And these rules, some of which were observed by the Church, had the effect of making men respect women during this time and allowing their bodies to renew themselves.

What is the actual role of blood in the Bible? Blood <u>cleanses</u>! It is life giving! <u>Trust</u> in Our <u>Heavenly Father's</u> design for our bodies. Blood keeps us alive but it also cleanses us. One reason that blood flows from a cut is to remove any impurities that might hurt our bodies. In the same way, our flow is the natural way to cleanse our insides, and it's usually painless.

So although we can initially be repelled by the thought of blood, or the sight of it, we need to remember that we are created by a perfect Designer Who invites us to work alongside Him in nurturing the human race.

Getting Gear

When we use the term "gear" we mean anything that helps collect menstrual flow either inside of our bodies or outside. The area between your legs which opens up to your body is very special and sensitive. This is why it is important to think about what products we put there. You want to use something that's good for you and good for the environment.

There are two kinds of gear for our cycle—items we use on the outside and things we use on the inside. It's very natural to begin with gear that is outside, but as you get older, you may prefer to use gear for the inside.

Items for the outside include pads and period panties. Pads can be made of plastic material or soft, natural cotton. There are many reusable options available! Reusable pads are made of cotton or flannel with a polyester backing to prevent leaking. Period panties provide complete coverage and can be used again and again. These items are usually most comfortable for young girls.

Gear that is used inside include tampons, sponges, and keeper cups. Because tampons are inserted into the vaginal canal, it's important to make sure they are as chemical-free as possible. Some come with paper or plastic applicators. Natural sponges are a reusable tampon that women have used for hundreds of years! They are inserted like a tampon and pulled out using a little string. Keeper cups are silicone cups which can be inserted and then taken out periodically throughout the day and reused.

Chemical-free products respect the natural balance of your body. Stay away from pads or tampons that have extra chemicals in them to "deodorize" or lock away moisture. These can cause yeast infections or irritate your vaginal area. Try to choose gear that is natural, chemical free, and (if possible) reusable.

No matter what you choose to use during menstruation, make sure you dispose of used items correctly. Wrap disposable pads or tampons in toilet paper and throw them in the trash. NEVER flush any menstrual items, including applicators, down the toilet. They will all find their way into our rivers and seas, and that is just gross! Reusable pads or panties usually come with a small zippered bag that you can wrap your items up in until they are washed. Being clean and responsible is a way to honor God and the environment He has given us!

PSALM 139:13-16

For it was You who formed my inward parts;
You knit me together in my mother's womb.

I praise You, for I am fearfully and wonderfully made. Wonderful are Your works; that I know very well.

My frame was not hidden from You, when I was being made in secret, intricately woven in the depths of the earth.

Your eyes beheld my unformed substance. In Your book were written all the days that were formed for me, when none of them as yet existed.

Mom, get ready to share your story!

During this activity, your daughter will be given the chance to interview you about your experiences with your first cycles. If you have some helpful or humorous stories to share, prepare them!

Some of us have not been taught to see the goodness of a woman's cycle. If this was true of you, share this honestly with your daughter, but also ask yourself: what caused you to change? Is this course giving you a new perspective? How can you help your daughter develop a good perspective on God's plan for womanhood?

This sharing is very important, so please take some time to think about it. As we know, so often our daughters' cycle will mirror our own, including any problems we might have had. We don't want to give our daughters fear, but we want to give them helpful information.

Here are the questions from her book for you:

- When did you start your cycle? How old were you?
- What was it like for you? How did you feel?
- Do you still have your cycle? If not, when did you stop having it?
- Have you ever had any problems with your cycle?

You can fill in the chart on gear for your cycle together, talking about the pros and cons of each one from your perspective.

The Care and Feeding of Emotions

Throughout a woman's life, we go through lots of changes and ups and downs. This is not some mistake that God made when He designed us—He made us this way on purpose! As our bodies go through cycles, this affects us not just physically, but emotionally as well. It is good for us to be aware of this connection between our bodies and our feelings because that will enable us to bring our entire being to our Heavenly Father and grow in our relationship with Him at every stage.

> "Therefore, behold, I will allure her, and bring her into the wilderness, and speak tenderly to her."
>
> **HOSEA 2:1**

What are hormones?

Hormones are the chemical messengers in your body that communicate and coordinate processes to your organs and tissues. Some of the things hormones regulate include digesting your food, regulating your body temperature, sleeping, and even just sensing what's going on around you. Hormones tell your body when to grow and when to start puberty. And as you guessed, hormones are part of your cycle as well!

The two hormones particularly important in a woman's cycle are estrogen and progesterone. While both men and women have these hormones, these two are more prominent in women and in regulating their cycle.

Estrogen is the hormone that triggers ovulation. So during the spring and summer stages of your cycle, estrogen levels rise. The presence of more estrogen can make you feel upbeat and energetic. It also helps your body maintain healthy skin and hair!

The problem with estrogen is that when it drops off, so does your mood. The drop in estrogen during the luteal phase can make you feel sad or distressed.

The good thing is that the progesterone hormone is right there to help out. Its levels begin to rise to "catch" the falling estrogen. As progesterone levels rise they partner along with estrogen as you end your cycle and begin it again. Progesterone can make you feel calm. This hormone helps you feel emotionally balanced as it reduces stress and it helps your body process sugar.

When progesterone drops, you may feel sluggish, have increased appetite, and experience some cramps and muscle weakness. This happens right before menstruation, the "winter season" of your cycle.

It's important for girls and women to keep these two hormones in balance so that they can have healthy cycles, and you can do this with good food, exercise, and sleep. You can see the rise and fall of these two hormones like a dance created by God to enable this cycle to continue.

The Body/Feeling Connection

As you can see, the rise and fall of hormones can definitely have an effect on your moods! An important part of maturity is recognizing that God allows these mood swings to happen but they can't control us. A mature woman who is feeling depressed can't just stop doing her job or taking care of her children because her estrogen levels are dropping. It's important to recognize that these natural body processes can affect our mood, but we don't have to let them determine how we behave.

Do you know there are women who take medication to actually STOP their cycle? Instead of seeing the connection between their feelings and their body as a gift, they see it as something to be controlled or manipulated. Not respecting the design of our Heavenly Father simply leads to more problems, not less.

 *Spring* FOLLICULAR PHASE

How might you feel during this stage?

While this growing is going on, you may feel most "yourself" or feel upbeat and positive.

How can you take care of yourself during this stage?

Use your positivity to plan and think of new ways you can learn and grow. What new skills, experiences, or ideas would you like to explore? Write down your goals for the month and ask God to guide you in using your energy wisely.

Summer OVULATION

How might you feel during this stage?

You might feel particularly strong, energetic, and confident.

How can you take care of yourself during this stage?

You might feel bold and daring, in this phase so challenge yourself. Be aware that you might be tempted to do something rash or harmful, so be sure to use this "super power" wisely and make smart choices. Tackle a new piece of music, try out for the school play, set a new personal best on the athletic field, or reach out and make new friends.

 *Autumn*
LUTEAL PHASE

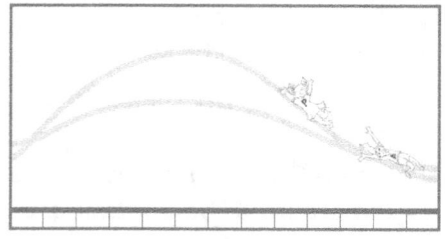

How might you feel during this stage?

You may feel a loss of energy and confidence or a mellowing of the strong feelings that you had. At the end of this phase you may even have feelings of sadness or discouragement as hormone levels fall and your body prepares for menstruation to begin.

How can you take care of yourself during this stage?

If you took on a challenge during the earlier stages, like you tried out for the school play and scored a big part, you might start feeling discouraged or overwhelmed. It's important to remember that you still have what it takes to complete that challenge. It's not like you suddenly became a bad actor or singer in just two weeks! This is a time to push through and remember that your confidence and enthusiasm will return before you know it.

At the end of this stage, you may begin to experience PMS, or premenstrual syndrome for a few days. PMS is characterized by physical and emotional symptoms. You may experience breast tenderness and slight cramping in your abdomen. Over-the-counter medication like ibuprofen may help. You also may feel down, sad, or discouraged. Recognize that these feelings may be related to what is going on inside of you at this time.

Make sure you are eating healthy during this stage, especially if you tend to binge when you are feeling low. Your body needs good nutritional support, so cut back on sugar and caffeine, and eat vitamin-rich foods you enjoy instead.

Winter
MENSTRUATION

How might you feel during this stage?

You may feel quiet, reflective and not very energetic. Feelings may tend to turn inward and may turn to sadness.

How can you take care of yourself during this stage?

Think of this cleansing time as a time of rest. Snuggle up like we do in wintertime. During your flow, try to take it easy, nourish yourself with healthy food, get a good night's sleep, and read good books. Winter doesn't have to be a depressing time: the days of your flow can be a time to step back, pray, think, connect with friends, and regain your focus on what's important.

If you have any discomfort during menstruation you can use a heating pad or hot water bottle on your tummy. Ibuprofen for a day or two will help along with the NORA tea suggested in Session 4. Avoid caffeine and sugar since these can make some unpleasant symptoms worse! Pay attention to what you eat and make sure to nourish your body during this time.

Tracking Your Cycle

Then just as spring follows winter, your body begins to build itself back up again. Your energy will build back up and your cleansed body will strengthen. You'll enter the follicular or growing stage of spring again, and the cycle will continue.

What is so beautiful about this cycle is that it just happens to us. We don't decide when it starts or stops: God decides. Embracing this cycle can make women in particular closer to our Creator God. We can start to recognize how He works: softly, gently, through our emotions, yet almost invisibly. Our Heavenly Father created us perfectly. We should praise Him for His wonderful design!

Learning to track your cycle is a wise idea. When you recognize how the seasons of your cycle can affect your mood, this can give you freedom!

When you track your cycle, it's easiest if you start with the ending: the winter or menstruation stage of your cycle. Even though it's the ending of the entire process, it's the part that's the most visible and hence the easiest to keep track of. Learning the signs of the other stages usually takes a longer time for most women, so when health professionals ask you about your cycle, they start with your period as stage one.

So here's the official medical order of a woman's cycle: winter, spring, summer, fall.

- Days 1-5 Menstruation (Winter)
- Days 6-11 Follicular (Spring)
- Days 12-16 Ovulation (Summer)
- Days 17-28 Luteal (Fall)

You'll notice that a woman's cycle is 28 days, but most calendar months are about 30 or 31 days. Interestingly, a woman's cycle is more similar to the lunar cycle—the cycle of the moon, which is about 28-29 days and contains four phases (new, half, full, half) just like a woman's cycle. In fact, the root word for menstruation, *mene*, is the Greek word for the moon.

> "It can thus be said that women, by looking to Mary, find in her the secret of living their femininity with dignity and of achieving their own true advancement."
>
> **REDEMPTORIS MATER, 5**

The moon has been special to women for this reason, and it's interesting to think of how the Church associates Our Lady with the moon. The moon glows because it reflects the light of the sun, and we honor and glorify Mary the Mother of God because she reflects the light of her Son: as she said, her whole being magnifies the greatness of the Lord! And even though she was also a teenage girl who had a cycle, it did not control her: she mastered it! This may be the reason why Scripture and many Catholic images portray Mary with the moon under her feet. When we reflect on this, we can draw closer to Our Lady during those times of the month when it's difficult.

My Personal Proverbs Chart

One tool we have found useful is the Personal Proverbs Chart created by Doran Richards. It is a way to both track your cycle and focus on a specific prayer intention for each stage. The chart uses the book of Proverbs from the Bible and four different colored markers. It's coded, so it's discreet if your chart is kept in a more public place.

1. For the season of **Menstruation**, we'll use the red marker, since red reminds us of blood and Christ's saving death. When Day 1 of your flow arrives, use a RED marker to write in "1" on that weekday and then read the first chapter of Proverbs. If any verse jumps out at you, read it again and think about what it means for your life. Write the number of the verse on that day of the chart. On Day 2, read the 2nd chapter of Proverbs, and repeat until your period is over. On each day, you could also mark if your flow is

heavy, medium or light. Reading your Proverbs will help you stay focused during this more difficult part of your cycle.

2. After your period is over, change the color to GREEN which stands for growing new life. This is the **Follicular Stage** or spring stage when your uterus is building a new lining and estrogen is climbing. Continue with numbering the days and recording the significant verses for yourself.

3. When you begin **Ovulation** (the Summer stage), change the color to PINK to represent joy and gladness. As the egg travels to your uterus, your estrogen will be peaking, so you may feel rather good. You will know you are ovulating when you notice mucus that is slippery, wet, or elastic. Continue with numbering the days and recording verses that speak to you.

4. When Ovulation is over, you will enter the **Luteal Phase** so you can start to write your numbers in ORANGE or YELLOW to stand for richness, abundance, and the fire of the Holy Spirit. This is the longest phase and at the end, you may experience some premenstrual signs which could be uncomfortable. Estrogen is decreasing so this may cause mood swings or feeling down. Use your chart and the Proverbs to develop extra focus as you work to cast on your burdens on the One Who cares for you.

Note: You may not get through all 31 chapters of the book of Proverbs every month and that's ok! The beauty of this exercise is that you will have the opportunity to read the Scriptures from a different perspective every time. You may choose to not start with Proverbs 1 on Day 1 every month so you can occasionally get through to the end of the book. Just keep track by writing the chapter you are reading on your chart.

Enter more fully into hearing God's word and plan through using this tool!

Managing Your Emotions

Let's talk about emotions. The emotions unleashed by your cycle can feel like God has just given you a large unruly animal and told you to keep it as a pet. Sometimes emotions can feel like you are managing a huge, energetic puppy! You might wonder how God can possibly ask you to manage something so crazy. But the good news is that He will always help us when we ask.

Emotions are terrible <u>masters</u>. They will make you miserable if you leave them in charge. But they are fantastic <u>pets</u>. Sometimes it helps to think of yourself like someone you have to take care of. If you realize you're getting upset and tearful, ask yourself if it's really true that everyone hates you, or if maybe your hormones are crashing and you just need to pray and take a nap.

Three Things

This is a great exercise when you are worrying about things in the future or something that happened in the past. We need to take time to focus on the present. That is where we are and where God is!

- **Notice three things that you see.** Look around you and see the details and colors in the items that are around you.

- **Notice three things that you hear.** If it's quiet maybe you hear the wind, or distant cars, or birds.

- **Notice three things that you physically feel.** Maybe it's your clothing, where you are sitting, or the air on your face.

- Repeat as needed to regain focus and peace.

Happy Place

- Close your eyes and take a few deep breaths.

- **Think of the feeling you want to have.** Do you want to be happy? Excited? Calm? Energized?

- **Now imagine a place where you would feel that way.** Think of a setting that evokes the feelings that you would like to have. It could be a real place like a forest or a beach or it could be an imaginary place.

- What are the things that you see? What are the sounds that you hear? What do you feel like?

- **Now take a "snapshot" of this memory.** When we do this, we can go back to that picture to evoke these feelings whenever you would like to.

Life would be boring without emotions, but we can't let them rule us! It's easy to get fooled by them. We must learn to manage them and to know what they are telling us. Actually, a women's connection to her emotions is a great gift and this connection is actually a great <u>gift</u> to the world.

Anxiety

When your levels of estrogen or progesterone go down, one side effect can be a feeling of anxiety. Some girls begin to worry about their appearance: they might feel ugly or out of place. Others might feel social anxiety: they are afraid of interacting with others or might wonder if their friends really like them. Other girls may worry about what is happening in their bodies as these changes occur. All of this is very understandable, but we need to learn how to take responsibility for our response to these feelings. This is part of the maturation that comes with womanhood.

Let's talk about fear or anxiety from a physiological point of view.

God made our brains to sense danger and respond accordingly. When <u>danger</u> is perceived, our brains <u>initiate a series of reactions</u> that increase our <u>heart rate</u>, <u>tighten the chest</u>, <u>raise our blood pressure</u>, <u>increase sweating</u>, and make us have <u>tunnel vision</u> where all we can see is the danger.

Anxiety occurs any time your brain receives a threat and sends the message to the body that you are not safe! You could be sitting at home on the couch, but your body could be responding as if there were a bear chasing you! These reactions would be helpful if there *were* a bear chasing you, but if there isn't, and your brain is just reacting to a "perceived threat"—that is anxiety.

We can speak truth to ourselves, be mindful of the present moment, and ourselves what is real. We can be present and change our feelings by changing our <u>thoughts</u>.

If there is no immediate danger to threaten us in the present moment, we can speak truth to ourselves, and that truth can then cause the opposite <u>reactions</u> in our body. As we calm down, our heart rate decreases, blood pressure decreases, and our mind broadens its focus to take in everything going on around us instead of focusing on one point.

Just as exercises are good for our physical health, there are also exercises that are good for our mental health. And the more we do them, the better we get at it! Taking charge of our brain and choosing what to think about helps us take control of our emotions.

Social Media: Warning!

One huge cause of anxiety in girls is social media. Apps like Facebook, Instagram, Tik Tok and others are designed to make people compare themselves to others and to make the users (that's you!) emotionally dependent upon the reactions of other people. This is not healthy or good. Research has shown very clearly that social media has a detrimental effect on the mental health of pre-teen and teenage girls.

We highly suggest no social media use at all until you are out of high school. Just as drinking alcohol or smoking when your body is growing and changing hurts your development physically, so does social media use hurt you as you are developing <u>socially</u> and <u>emotionally</u>. When you are an adult, you will have more of a capacity to use social media without it affecting you as much, because you will have completed most of your social development as a teen.

Find other ways to connect with friends through <u>texts</u>, <u>phone calls</u>, or <u>social events</u>. You don't need to have hundreds of friends to feel wanted and loved. Your family and close friends who really know and love you are enough!

When to Get Help

If you are truly struggling with your emotions at any time—if you notice that your sadness is preventing you from <u>doing things you like</u>—treat yourself the way you would treat a friend, and get help! You wouldn't let a friend struggle alone in the dark, so get help for yourself. Ask <u>your mom</u> or a close woman relative to help you figure out what's going on. Most of us have been there, and sometimes a severe mood swing can be a signal that something physical is going on that needs to be addressed.

Certainly if you or a friend ever have thoughts of hurting yourself, you should <u>tell your parents immediately</u>. Talk about suicide or self-harm should always be taken seriously. If someone you know is tempted by thoughts of suicide or who talks about hurting themselves in any way, talk to your mom immediately, even if your friend asks you not to.

If you need it, the national suicide prevention number to call or text for help is 988.

The Importance of Prayer

For many women, our cycle demonstrates to us the truth that we can't control everything in our lives. What we can control is our response. This can open us up to God and we can ask Him to step in. Again, this is an invitation from God to women to draw closer to Him.

It's important to be thankful for the good people and good things in our lives. It's important to remember who we are and Who our God is. That's one reason why we should take time to pray every day. Just spending fifteen minutes a day in your room alone to talk and listen to God can make a huge difference in your life.

> "The difficulties of life do not have to be unbearable. It is the way we look at them— through faith or unbelief—that makes them seem so. We must be convinced that our Father is full of love for us and that He only permits trials to come our way for our own good."
>
> **BROTHER LAWRENCE,**
> ***THE PRACTICE OF THE PRESENCE OF GOD***

Here are some scriptures for you to look up and read to help you understand how much our Heavenly Father loves us and cares for us.

- Psalm 56:3
- Phillippians 4:6-7
- John 14:27
- 2 Timothy 1:7
- 1 John 4:18
- Psalm 94:19
- Isaiah 43:1
- Psalm 23:4

PSALM 139:1-4, 23-24

O Lord, You have searched
me and known me.
You know when I sit down
and when I rise up;
You discern my thoughts
from far away.

You search out my path
and my lying down,
and are acquainted
with all my ways.

Even before a word
is on my tongue,
O Lord, You know
it completely....

...Search me, O God,
and know my heart;
test me and know
my thoughts.

See if there is any
wicked way in me,
and lead me in the
way everlasting.

Mom, get ready to share your story!

In this interview, your daughter will ask you how you managed mood swings or your emotions during your cycle. You might want to think over your life and how you have managed your emotions. Was there a time you thought your life was falling apart, only to realize you were experiencing a bad case of PMS? When did you realize that, and how did that affect your strategies in the future? Do you have any funny stories to share?

Think about your relationship with God. This is a great time for you to reflect on your own relationship with God so you can guide your daughter. Think of some of your favorite scriptures or saints that you would like to share with her.

Here are the questions from her book for you:

- Do/did your moods change during your cycle?
- How did you take care of yourself during your cycle?
- What place does prayer have in your life?
- Do you have a favorite scripture?

Let's Talk About Change

When we begin our cycle, it's not just our insides that change: it's many other things outside as well! God prepares our bodies in many ways for the great work of bringing new life into the world. This means that we grow taller and stronger: our breasts which are used to nurse babies will grow larger. The parts of our bodies that are involved in giving birth grow protective hair. This means we need to take extra care of our bodies and treat them with the respect they deserve.

The following changes may not happen to you all at once. They happen little by little over four to six years. Some changes might affect you a lot while others might be no big deal. Every girl and woman is different!

Remember that Our Lady also experienced these changes as she grew from a girl into a woman. These changes aren't gross or dirty, but they are profound and indicate we have a new responsibility. Up until now, our parents have taken care of us. Now we need to begin to take care of ourselves, because someday, we will be taking care of others.

> "When the body is seen as mere matter, anything goes. The body, however, isn't mere matter. That's modernist fiction. Rather, as the Catholic anthropology of the theology of the body reminds us, man is a union of body and soul, made in the image of God. Which means our bodies are us. Your body is you. My body is me."
>
> **EMILY STIMPSON**
> **THESE BEAUTIFUL BONES, PG 27**

The world will tell you your body is just atoms and molecules, and that what you do with it is your business. But this is a lie. Our bodies are not our own. They belong to God and we need to take care of them.

Let's approach these conversations with the knowledge that as our bodies change, WE change. The Lord is forming your heart and mind and your body during this time, and His plan is designed for your happiness and wholeness. The Scripture challenges us to be transformed by the renewal of our minds as we contemplate God's plan and design.

Breast Development

THE CHANGE: BREASTS BEGIN TO GROW

About two to three years before their cycles begin, girls begin to develop breasts. It's important to take care of your breasts, and this is where bras become important. During this time of development, your breasts may become tender. Don't worry if they aren't exactly the same size. This is all very normal!

YOUR RESPONSE: WEAR A GOOD BRA

Bras can help with your <u>posture</u>. For women with large breasts, they give important back support. A bra that fits you well makes it easier for you to stand up straight with your shoulders back.

Bras <u>protect</u> your <u>breasts</u>, and breasts need protection. If you play sports, a good bra is essential to shield your breasts. They can bruise if they're jostled or bounced around too much. Also, when your cycle begins, your breasts might feel more tender at some times than others. A good bra provides protection and support.

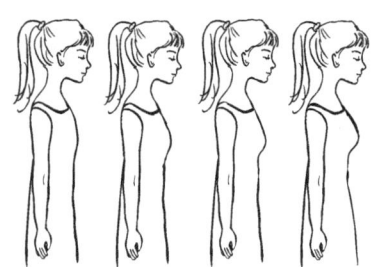

Bras also protect your <u>modesty</u>. A bra that fits you should cover the sides of your breast as well as your cleavage. Be sure it is thick enough to keep your nipples in. Nipples popping out can look odd and be distracting to others, and be aware that nipples can become hard if you're cold or super-excited. A good bra should smooth these out and make you look more attractive.

Speaking of nipples, occasionally a young woman's nipples will not pop out of her breast, but will remain flat or inverted like a belly button. This can cause problems with breastfeeding babies later on, and might just be a sign of another underlying medical problem, so if you notice this problem, be sure to tell your mom.

Bras just make you look more <u>attractive</u>. When you move, your breasts shouldn't be moving separately or jiggle around. People should also not be able to see your bra through your clothing or see your bra strap hanging out. A well-fitting bra will give you smooth lines around your body and will make your clothing and your body more pleasant to look at.

When should I begin wearing a bra? As girls begin to develop breasts, they should start by wearing an undershirt and then a half shirt with a little padding. Many girls like to start with a sports bra or what used to be called a "training bra." But as the breasts grow, it's important to keep shopping and find a bra that fits you well. It's ideal to have about <u>3-5</u> bras in your wardrobe.

A good quality bra may last about <u>a year</u>. The elastic used to construct them can deteriorate in the dryer, so it's useful to air dry them. Hang them in a hanger in your closet to dry. If your bra is itchy, uncomfortable, makes your back or shoulders ache, or starts to show through your clothing, it's probably not the right size, or no longer fits you well. Ask your mother to help you find one that fits you well and supports you.

More hair, everywhere! (not really)

THE CHANGE: NEW HAIR GROWTH

As our bodies change, you will notice that hair begins to grow in new places. You may discover darker hair growing on your <u>legs</u>, in your <u>armpits</u>, or between your legs over your <u>vaginal area</u>. This hair, called pubic hair, is there for a reason: to protect what is precious. Pubic hair is very sensitive and difficult to shave off, so think of it as a sort of hedge to protect this opening into your body.

YOUR RESPONSE: A SHAVING ROUTINE

If the hair on your legs or armpits bothers you or looks strange, ask your mom to teach you how to shave them. In our culture, most women shave their armpits and legs. Shaving works best if it's done after a shower or warm bath, using soap to shave and a body polish afterwards. Once or twice a week works for most young women. Shaving the pubic area isn't recommended since the hair protects these bodily openings from infection, but you can carefully cut longer strands if they bother you. If your swimsuit isn't covering your pubic hair, switch to one with more coverage.

Sweet Scents

THE CHANGE: BODY ODOR

The hormones that are changing your body into an adult body can also cause more sweat and in particular, can give you an unpleasant body odor. Of all the signs that puberty is beginning, often your body odor is what family members might notice first (and comment on). This is true for both boys and girls!

YOUR RESPONSE: INCREASED CLEANLINESS AND PLEASANT SCENTS

It is usually during this time of change that women start bathing or showering more often, sometimes every day. You may also choose to shower every other day. This is the best solution to the increased odors that your body may emit.

Deodorant is important and may be necessary if you are involved in physical activity such as sports or a hard-working job. Find a deodorant whose smell you like that uses natural ingredients like shea butter or aloe. Try to avoid deodorants labeled anti-perspirants which block sweat or ones containing ingredients like aluminum or synthetics, since all of these can interfere with a woman's hormones. Apply deodorant under your armpits daily on dry skin before leaving the house. Some women with large breasts use it under their breasts as well.

Another thing many women do is discover a perfume or other fragrance that they use on a regular basis. This can become your very own "signature scent"! Fragrances come in many scents, from floral to woody to citrus to spicy and range from dollar-store varieties to decorative bottles worth thousands of dollars. (What's the difference? Better quality scents contain more oils so you use less of them, and their scents can last 12 hours or more.) Ask your mom to help you find a fragrance that's affordable and fits your age and personality.

So body odor isn't the end of the world: it might be the beginning of your exploration of the enchanting world of scents!

Skin Changes (the least fun part of growing up)

THE CHANGE: INCREASED OIL ON THE SKIN FROM HORMONAL CHANGES

Another sign of puberty is your skin producing more oil, especially on your face and the upper part of your body. When this oil clogs your pores, this can cause pimples or patches of red raised bumps. Pimples can swell and turn into whiteheads or blackheads or even cause scarring. This phenomenon is called acne. Acne is caused by hormones (again!) but is definitely affected by stress, cleanliness, and diet.

YOUR RESPONSE: AVOID STRESS, WASH YOUR FACE, EAT BETTER

If you struggle with acne, find a good skin cleanser that works with your skin type and use it daily. Start with a mild cleanser and moisturizer and see how your skin responds. It is a good idea to begin the habit of washing your face in the morning and before you go to bed when you brush your teeth. Be aware that serious acne may need the help of a dermatologist.

Since sugary, fatty, or greasy foods can trigger acne, you may want to try cutting out those foods from your diet. Acne may also be a sign of a food allergy or sensitivity. You can try giving up something you eat regularly and see if it makes any difference in your skin. Part of taking care of yourself is noticing how things affect you.

Sleeping Like a Baby

THE CHANGE: INCREASED FATIGUE

Your body is in a time of rapid change—physically and emotionally. You are learning new things and growing very quickly. These changes take up a lot of your energy! Also, your body's production of melatonin—a hormone that helps you sleep—changes. This means you may want to sleep later in the morning, and stay up at night.

Lack of sleep on a regular basis can make you <u>irritable, upset, anxious, or just foggy</u>. Losing sleep can <u>lower your immune system</u>, <u>affect your performance at school or in sports</u>, and your emotions *really* don't like being sleep-deprived.

THE SOLUTION: GET MORE SLEEP.

Studies say teenagers should get <u>8-10</u> hours of sleep a night. If you're getting less than that on a regular basis, talk to your parents about arranging your schedule to get more sleep. Teens need as much sleep as a toddler! Maybe taking afternoon naps can be arranged?

If you have trouble falling or staying asleep, tell your parents and check your screentime and diet. Be sure to <u>keep electronics, especially phones and tablets, out of your room</u> when you are going to sleep since their lights or super-sonic noises can disrupt sleep cycles. And you don't want to be kept awake by texts or distracted by online content when you should be sleeping.

Start the habit of <u>reading the Bible</u> as you fall asleep or <u>praying the Rosary</u>. If you are thinking about a problem or worrying about something, make an effort to <u>give that to God, and trust He will help you</u>. Psalm 127:2 reminds us "For He takes care of His beloved ones even while they sleep."

Growing: A Good Excuse to Go Shopping!

THE CHANGE: GROWTH IN SHOE SIZE, HEIGHT, AND WEIGHT

The first sign that changes are coming in your body very often is when the shoes you bought three months ago all of the sudden do not fit. This can be annoying to you and frustrating for your mom who needs to go shopping all over again! You may also feel clumsy and awkward as you get used to your adult body. This happens because your feet grow first, and then your body grows. It's ok to feel like you have "big feet" for a bit, but do not worry: your body will catch up and you will be exactly the size you are meant to be!

> Take a minute to practice standing with a good posture. Stand with your feet parallel and directly below your hips. Take time to feel your feet and balance your weight evenly across them. Your shoulders, hips and ankles should all be in a straight line. Lengthen your neck and think of making space between your head and your pelvis. Make sure you stand with your shoulders down and back. Simply standing tall can lift our mood and make us feel more confident!

YOUR RESPONSE: BE CONFIDENT AND GET NEW CLOTHES!

As we get taller, some girls tend to lose the good posture they had when they were a child. So <u>practice good posture</u>! Keeping good body alignment not only shows confidence when you relate to others, but it is good for your muscles and internal organs.

As you grow, take some time to <u>go shopping</u> with your mom, but be aware that you may grow out of those shoes or clothes in just a few months, so spend wisely! Make sure you get rid of clothes that don't fit to make room for new ones. **(More about clothes and fashion coming in Session 5!)**

Body Image and the Lilies of the Field

Have you ever considered the beauty of a flower? If you were asked to picture a flower in your mind, it would probably be different from the flower your mom or dad or friends would picture. Why? Because all flowers are <u>different</u>, but they each have a <u>unique</u> beauty that is all their own. The same God Who designed thousands of different flowers fashioned *you* with a particular beauty that no one else will ever have. Each of us has been perfectly created by our Heavenly Father, though all of our bodies are different.

It is important to thank God for how He designed and fashioned you. Thank Him for your eye color, hair color, skin tone, height, weight, and everything about you. He made you uniquely beautiful and He expects you to care for yourself. Sometimes women choose to dye their hair, pierce their ears, or work hard to lose weight or tone their muscles. We should do these things if our motivation is to honor and care for our bodies. But if in your heart you want to punish yourself or show hatred for your body, this is wrong. When considering how we treat our bodies, ask yourself: does it show reverence for the gift God gave me?

It's good to be aware of the images that we see in our culture of women and an unhealthy unrealistic pursuit of "the perfect look." This is another reason that living online and using social media is so harmful to young women. Constantly <u>comparing</u> ourselves to filtered, photoshopped images doesn't help anyone appreciate their unique body. Make sure that you <u>care</u> for your body in a way that <u>honors</u> your unique design, and then learn how you can appreciate the beauty in other people without <u>jealousy</u> or <u>envy</u>.

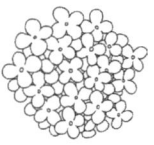
Hydrangea

Allium

Peony

Anemone

Buttercup

Carnation

Star
of Bethlehem

Rose

PSALM 139: 7-12

Where can I go from
Your spirit?
Or where can I flee
from Your presence?

If I ascend to heaven,
You are there;
if I make my bed in
Sheol, You are there.

If I take the wings
of the morning
and settle at the farthest
limits of the sea,

even there Your hand
shall lead me,
and Your right hand
shall hold me fast.

If I say, "Surely the
darkness shall cover me,
and the light around
me become night,"

even the darkness is
not dark to You;
the night is as bright
as the day,
for darkness is as
light to You.

Mom, get ready to share your story!

Think about yourself when you were your daughter's age. So much has changed, hasn't it? Instead of just sharing your story, find a picture of yourself when you were her age. Make a copy of it or print it out so you can give it to her for her workbook. It would be great to even find pictures of older sisters, aunts, or even grandmothers to share with her! The idea is to communicate to your daughter that she is not alone in going through these changes. You went through them and so did all the women she knows!

In your daughter's book she has some interview questions for you. Here they are so you can start thinking now what your answers will be!

When you were your daughter's age....

- Who was your best friend?
- What was your favorite ice cream?
- What were you really good at?
- What was your favorite color?
- What did you do with your friends?
- What was your favorite thing to wear?

What of these things has changed? What has stayed the same?

After this conversation, we want to encourage you to help your daughter choose a flower that represents her unique beauty. There are so many flowers to choose from! This could be a special symbol for the two of you for this course, but also for the rest of her life. See her book for some guidance on how she can do this. The best choice for her will be the flower that SHE chooses. Feel free to ask guiding questions and offer suggestions, but allow her to express herself however she feels most comfortable. Every flower is beautiful!

Caring for our Body, a Temple of the Holy Spirit

Let's take a deep dive into how to take care of yourself through diet, exercise, and hydration. Remember that because you are young, it's easier for you to start making healthy changes for yourself. The choices you make today can form habits for a lifetime!

There's a chart at the end of this chapter in your daughter's book for her to fill out. The first three rows are review: see what she remembers from previous chapters! Yes, it's ok for her to peek! That's how we learn and remember.

> "Do you not know that your body is a temple of the Holy Spirit within you, which you have from God? You are not your own; you were bought with a price. So glorify God in your body."
>
> **1 CORINTHIANS 19:20**

Nutrition

Have you heard the saying, "You are what you eat?" As you grow, the food you eat becomes part of your body, and if it's good food, your body will be stronger and last longer. But if your food is poor, your lifelong health can be damaged. As a young girl, your adult body is being created right now through the food choices you make, and things are changing fast!

As you grow into an adult, you're going to start choosing your own foods, and it's really important that you start making healthy choices. The choices you make affect your brain, so if you choose to eat healthy, your brain and taste buds will start enjoying healthy food. But if you keep eating sugar and candy and empty calories, your brain will become addicted to them and keep craving them. Remember how we learned how you are in charge of your emotions: your emotions are not in charge of you? You have to do a similar thing with your brain and your taste buds!

Learning about macronutrients

Macronutrients include <u>carbohydrates</u>, <u>proteins</u>, and <u>fats</u>. Some foods are pure carbs, proteins or fats, but most foods are a mixture. Seeds and nuts can contain both carbs and protein, and most meat and dairy have both fat and protein. There are healthy and unhealthy fats as well: sometimes called unsaturated and saturated fats.

A great way to build a healthy diet is to build a healthy plate. At every meal try to fill half of your plate fruits and vegetables, a quarter with proteins, and a quarter with whole grains. For growing girls, you should make sure you get enough calcium from food like dairy products, but also legumes and nuts. This is a great time to start learning to cook and helping your family by cooking for them. You may be meal-planning feeding your own family someday!

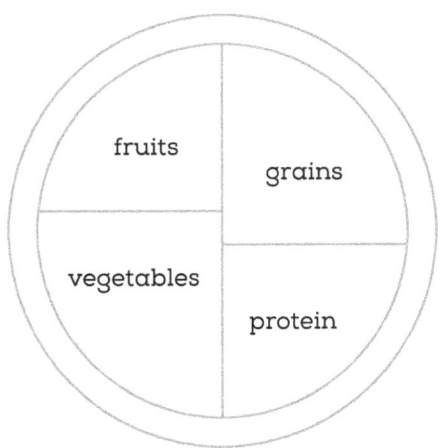

A variety of macronutrients in a meal means your plate will contain a variety of natural colors! Learning to eat a variety of foods helps you to enjoy the wide range of foods that God created to nourish and sustain our bodies.

Portion size: everything in moderation

Make a <u>fist</u>. That's about the size that your stomach should be, and the amount of food your stomach can hold. When we eat too much food on a regular basis, our stomach can stretch out and leave us feeling hungry for more food than we need. The good thing is that we can readjust the size of our stomach by eating less.

Incidentally, if you don't eat enough food on a regular basis, your stomach can shrink too much, and the acid contained in your stomach can start to creep up your esophagus, causing chest pain, nausea, and other problems. And not eating enough food can cause lots of other problems as well, including death by starvation! So it's important to eat regularly and healthily to keep your stomach its correct size: the size of your closed fist.

GET A "HAND"-LE ON PORTION CONTROL

Palm: 3-4 oz of meat, salty snacks or whole grains

Fist: 1 cup of veggies

Tip of finger: teaspoon of salt, oil or butter

Thumb: 2 tablespoons of healthy fats

Now open your hand, and look at the palm. There's a measuring guide built into your hand as well! The size of your palm is roughly the size of about 3-4 ounces of meat. So if you're cutting yourself a slice of pork loin or chicken breast at the dinner table, that's about how much you want: the size of your palm. If you're indulging in a salty snack like pretzels or chips, that's about the maximum you should eat, too.

The size of your clenched fist is about a cup. Try to eat a cup of leafy greens or raw vegetables at each meal. Two scoops of ice cream is also about one cup, and one scoop is a half cup. The front of your fist is also a good half-cup measure, and you should eat about half cup of things like cooked vegetables, diced fruit, or pasta.

The top section of your finger is about the size of a teaspoon, so use that to measure how much butter or oil to put on your bread or salad. About one teaspoon of salt per day is all you need to be healthy: more salt than you need can make you bloated, thirsty, or cause long-term, more serious diseases.

When you prepare a meal for yourself, try using a smaller plate so you can fill it up. Be aware that most restaurants serve over-large portions, so when you go out to eat, plan on eating only half of what you're served, or share a plate with a friend or family member.

The Church recommends fasting as a spiritual practice, especially for men and adults. Some of us find fasting easier than others. At this time in your life, try fasting from eating between meals and from unhealthy snacks. That's usually enough of a penance for most of us!

Nutrient Dense vs. Energy Dense

There is a difference between foods that give you energy and foods that give you nutrients. Nutrients like proteins, carbohydrates, fats, minerals, and vitamins are what your body needs to build itself up. When you are growing, you need to focus on foods that give you good nutrients.

Foods that give you energy but are poor nutritionally include things like sugary drinks, fried foods like potato chips, cookies, candy, soda, and packaged processed foods with tons of ingredients. These might give you energy and taste great, but can cause problems.

Here's another comparison: two breakfast plates.

One plate contains a cup of coffee with cream, a small bowl of low-sugar cereal with sliced banana, a cup of fruit, a piece of wheat toast with a teaspoon of jelly, an egg, and a link sausage. Sound amazing? By using low-carb options, that breakfast would only cost you 500 calories. Not only does it contain every macronutrient family with minerals, vitamins, good fats, and fiber, but it's inviting and fun to eat, and will give you energy for a long time.

The second plate is two chocolate donuts and a mug of coffee. Also 500 calories, but they're basically worthless. This breakfast might give you a quick energy boost, but you'll soon crash and feel hungry again after eating it. Worst of all, the extra energy you didn't use will be stored as fat.

We need to regularly choose healthy nutrient-rich foods over empty calories, and pick the healthy foods most often.

How to Make Healthy Choices

The food industry creates highly processed foods like cereals, bars, and other products which don't spoil easily and can be stored a long time, so they're cheaply priced. That's great if you need a snack on a trip where you can't cook or refrigerate anything. The problem is that these foods are often stripped of most of their nutrients and contain salt, sugar, and fats. Also artificial ingredients are used to preserve them, so processed foods shouldn't be eaten on a regular basis.

The good news is that there is a lot of variety among fresh foods, so go exploring! Try new fruits or vegetables or find ways to cook the ones you already eat so that you enjoy them more. Learn to make lunch and dinner salads, or how to bake and cook your own foods from basic ingredients so you can enjoy a cake or cookie as a treat that doesn't contain weird preservatives. Certain foods are very good for women's health, and those foods include vegetables and fruits that give important minerals that are needed during your cycle. So find ways to enjoy these foods that are needed by your body.

Supporting Your Cycle

Use this chart to help your daughter fill out the worksheet on p. 54 of her book. If you're wondering how you can support your cycle through your diet, here's a helpful chart from Alisa Vitti's book *In the Flo: Unlock Your Hormonal Advantage and Revolutionize Your Life* (Harper Collins, 2021).

	FOLLICULAR PHASE	OVULATION	LUTEAL PHASE	MENSTRUATION
EAT	pumpkin or flax seeds	corn	sunflower/ sesame seeds	proteins
	oats	tomatoes	brown rice	kale
	carrots	almonds	celery/sweet potatoes	blueberries
	avocados	dark chocolate	dark chocolate	decaf coffee
	cashews	strawberries	cucumbers	
	chicken	salmon	apples/bananas	
			beef/turkey	
			peppermint	

Rethink Your Drink

Studies are showing that most of our extra sugar (and salt!) is not in food that we eat, but in the liquids we drink. Sugar isn't nutritionally necessary for our bodies and too much of it is harmful. What used to be a treat is now a bad habit for too many people, and most of our sugar intake is sneaking into our drinks. Juices and sodas are fine every once in a while, but not something to drink daily or whenever we feel thirsty. The same rules for processed foods apply to drinks: many pre-bottled drinks, even diet ones, contain lots of preservatives and artificial ingredients that are bad for us.

We need to drink regularly, and most of us aren't getting all the hydration we need. So it's worthwhile examining what you drink and making healthier choices.

Milk (and Vitamin D)

One nutrient you need as a young growing woman is calcium, especially calcium fortified with Vitamin D. From now until your mid-20s, you are building your bones, which require those two macros. After you reach about age 25, your bones will stop growing, and if you don't maintain them with regular calcium intake, they'll start deteriorating. So as a growing woman, look for ways to have calcium on a daily basis to build

The Properties of the the Herbs in NORA tea

NETTLES

- Removes toxins in blood
- Regulates blood sugar
- Anti-inflammatory so eases menstrual cramps
- Contains most absorbable form of calcium
- High in iron, silica, potassium, calcium, & vitamin K which all help control bleeding

OATSTRAW

- Calming to the nerves
- Improves mood by supporting your nervous system
- Strengthens uterus
- Aids in sleep
- helps hormone balancing
- Soothes the digestive system
- Enhances calcium absorption

RED RASPBERRY LEAF

- Helps relax the uterus which aids in menstrual cramps
- Tones uterus which helps control bleeding
- Contains the most absorbable form of calcium
- Soothes kidneys & urinary tract
- Stabilizes digestive tract

ALFALFA

- Increases urine production to help remove toxins
- Rich in trace minerals like iron
- Purifies the blood
- Soothes the digestive tract
- Balances intestinal bacteria

stronger, longer-lasting bones. The easiest way to do this is to drink about three cups of Vitamin D milk a day.

If you don't care for milk or can't have it, look for other ways to get calcium such as yogurt or cheeses. As for Vitamin D, you can get that from going outside on a sunny day—about ten minutes in spring and summer and longer in the wintertime. Vitamin D sunshine gives you a good excuse to spend time outside as much as possible doing sports, activities or just hanging out and doing homework.

Water

Water is essential for life. Humans can survive up to three months without food, but we can only survive three days without water! Water is the main component of blood which carries nutrients to all our body parts and gets rid of waste. Healthy blood means a healthy body! Water helps us keep a constant temperature when it is very hot or cold, it provides a cushion for our brain and all our joints, and relieves stress from our heart as it pumps blood throughout the body.

Water also helps us to think clearly which enables us to control our emotions and regulate our feelings. Many of the side effects of dropping hormones are also things that are exacerbated by lack of water. Staying hydrated helps with the symptoms of water retention, muscle cramps, headaches, and fatigue.

How does this affect your cycle? When you are menstruating, your body is losing fluids that need to be replaced! Drinking enough water ensures that your body has what it needs during this important time.

Hydration also helps prevent urinary tract infections and keeps the balance of pH levels and healthy bacteria in your vaginal area. When a woman is pregnant or nursing, water is super-necessary to keep her and her baby healthy. If you are healthily hydrated, when you use the bathroom, your pee should be a light yellow color. If it is dark, like the color of the McDonalds "M", you should drink more water!

So start on the habit of drinking water. Buy a water bottle that you like—maybe with a straw or a spill-proof lid. Make it personal by decorating it with stickers or bright colors. If you don't like plain water, flavor it with a slice of lemon, a bit of cranberry juice or grapefruit. Do what works for you! This is a habit that if developed when you are young, will serve you for a lifetime!

Herbal Teas

Aside from vegetables and macronutrient plants, there are other plants God created which we usually don't eat alone but use in other ways. These plants—called herbs—have savory, aromatic, or medicinal properties that can make our food taste better, create healthy fragrances, or maintain or heal our bodies! You can buy herbs at the store, but many of them are easy to grow or even find in the wild or your own backyard. There are thousands of herbs to explore, but here are a few common ones that are healthy for a woman's cycle and easy to grow yourself if you're interested. It's amazing that God has provided not only food to nourish us but herbs to support the normal processes of our womanly bodies.

We use most of these herbs as teas by drying the leaves, crushing them, and adding them to water, hot or cold, so the herbal nutrients can be easily absorbed into the body. Learning about herbs can encompass a lifetime, and there are many options to explore. But when it comes to menstruation, our favorite tea is this simple but nourishing and easy-to-make NORA tea which relieves many common complaints during menstruation. It's called NORA after the names of the herbal ingredients: Nettles, Oatstraw, Red Raspberry Leaf, and Alfalfa.

Exercise

In our society, people rarely work outside, walk to destinations, or do heavy physical labor any longer. Because God meant for us to move and be active, this means that most of us have to exercise to keep our bodies strong and balanced. A good exercise program should include activities you enjoy as well as exercises that you don't enjoy, but which challenge you and make you stronger. Doing this builds discipline, and the discipline of exercise can build your strength to do things that aren't fun, like finishing your homework, being patient with family members, or managing your emotions.

Exercising during your cycle has a particular rhythm, and if you understand your cycle, you can pair each stage with exercises that work with your body instead of against it.

Additionally, exercise has strong emotional benefits. Just a brisk walk, a bike ride, a round of volleyball or even just a burst of jumping jacks can improve your mood, relieve stress and anxiety, help you focus, and make your sleep better. Sports and activities like dance or gymnastics also build skills, confidence, and connect you with other people. Studies have shown that conditions like ADHD and depression improve with as little as 20 minutes of regular exercise.

So let's look at the four seasons (in the official medical order) and helpful exercise for each stage. Daughters can use this page to fill out their chart on p. 54.

MENSTRUATION: WINTER

- Do stretches, especially if you're cramping: try sitting with your legs in a wide-leg straddle, do the "cobra" pose, the "bow" pose, or the "butterfly" position (the last opens up your hips by sitting with your heels pressed together and gently pulling them up to your hips with your hands).

- Do light cardiovascular exercise—running, jumping jacks, dancing.

- Work on your core: planks, squats, leg lifts, and other exercises.

- It's ok to just rest and recover.

Daughters can use this page to fill out their chart on p. 54.

HOW TO MAKE NORA TEA:

Combine:

- 2 parts nettle leaf,
- 1 part oatstraw,
- 2 parts raspberry leaves,
- and 1 part alfalfa leaves.

Store in a plastic ziplock bag, mason jar, or paper carton until you need it.

To make a cup of tea:

- put 1 teaspoon of tea into 1 cup of boiling water
- steep for 10 minutes.

Strain, sweeten with honey, and drink.

To make NORA iced tea:

- pour 1 quart of boiling water into 1 cup of tea
- steep for 20 - 30 min.
- strain out the tea leaves with a cheesecloth or tea strainer, then pour into a container.

Sweeten and add ice to serve.

FOLLICULAR: SPRING

- Try some cardio! Run, take a bike ride, go on a hike, organize a game of tag, soccer, or frisbee with friends.
- If you're already exercising, build your endurance: do your exercises for longer, include extra repetitions, run or walk further distances.
- Try weightlifting. Now is the best season to build muscle.

OVULATION: SUMMER

- If you're an athlete, this is your peak training time!
- Learn a new skill, perfect a current skill.

LUTEAL: FALL

- Move to lower intensity cardio: from running to walking or swimming.
- Do light strength training.
- Try pilates or other exercises that can ease cramps and strengthen your core.
- Build endurance.

When Things Go Wrong

We live in a world that was broken by sin, and that means that sometimes God's design does not work as it should. While most healthy women have no real difficulties with their cycle, there are a few conditions you should be aware of. If you experience any of these, tell your mother so that you can consult with a healthcare professional. Girls who track their cycle can catch many of these problems before they become serious, so it's good to learn what is and is not a serious symptom. **Note: "Menorrhea" is a Latin word that means "monthly flow," and you'll notice that many of the terms have that as a base.**

Amenorrhea

Amenorrhea means "No monthly flow," and it refers to a woman who has no menstruation, or no cycle at all. As you now know, that's kind of a problem.

It's normal for women who are pregnant, breastfeeding, or in menopause to not have periods (in fact, many mothers first discover they are pregnant when their period stops). However, this is abnormal in young girls and women and could be an indicator of underlying health issues.

When a growing girl fails to have a period by age 16, this is known as primary amenorrhea. Most girls enter puberty around age 11 or 12 or earlier, and have their cycle begin shortly afterwards. Girls who are underweight and highly athletic might not start their cycle at a normal time. If this describes you or someone you know, it's time to consult a doctor. Usually the problem is caused by a problem with the pituitary gland, hypothalamus, or ovaries.

If a girl or woman whose cycle has started stops having her cycle for more than three months, this is known as secondary amenorrhea. The causes might be nutritional changes, rapid changes in weight, strenuous exercise, stress, or an eating disorder. The loss of your cycle can be the first indicator that there is something more seriously wrong.

If you realize you have amenorrhea, here are three things you can do.

- **Start with your diet:** Are you eating properly? Are you eating too much or too little? Girls need to have the proper amount of healthy fat in their diet, and have a proper weight for their height.

- **Look at your activity levels:** Are you working too hard or doing too much? Losing your cycle is often a warning to female athletes that they need to slow down or work more wisely.
- **Third, try to reduce the stress in your life.** Sometimes emotional conflict can impact our health! Talk to your parents or a mentor to try to resolve what is causing you stress.

Dysmenorrhea

"Dys" means painful or abnormal. So dysmenorrhea refers to having extreme pain or discomfort during menstruation. Most women experience some discomfort, but dysmenorrhea is pain that is out of the ordinary. One reason for dysmenorrhea is overproduction of the hormone prostaglandins, which helps the uterus contract. The most obvious symptom is "Killer Cramps" that do not respond to normal self-care or ibuprofen and cause you to miss school, work, or other activities. A woman may also experience headaches, diarrhea, constipation, frequent urination, or even fainting.

Here are some things that may help:
- Take ibuprofen or naproxen sodium.
- Use a heating pad or hot water bottle for cramps.
- Eat food with Omega 3s, vitamin A, and magnesium.
- Get adequate sleep.

If the above remedies don't give any relief, its very important that you consult a health care professional to see if you might have fibroids or endometriosis.

Fibroids are benign tumors in the uterus that can cause pain and increased bleeding when the uterus contracts against them during menstruation. They are rare in teens but more common in women over 30. African-American women are more at risk for developing painful fibroids as they age, and so are women who are obese or who take artificial hormones. Painful fibroids can be removed by surgery, or managed by medication and lifestyle changes.

Menorrhagia

"Rhagia" means bursting in Latin, so menorrhagia is heavy, abnormal bleeding, different from the normal menstrual bleeding of 1-5 tablespoons. If your period lasts longer than 5 days, if you soak a regular pad in an hour several hours at a time, or if you frequently have to change pads or tampons in the middle of the night, you may have menorrhagia.

Menorrhagia might be caused by thyroid issues, low rates of progesterone, fibroids, polyps in the endometrium, or another bleeding disorder. As you can see, that's a wide range for your health care professional to evaluate. But they will usually start asking you about your diet, so be sure you are eating healthy.

Irregular Bleeding

A normal cycle should be a regular cycle. But if as you chart, you discover that you are bleeding in between periods or that your periods are less than 21 days apart and more than 45 days apart, have a professional look into it. The causes of an irregular cycle can vary, but it can be caused by imbalances in hormones or problems in your organs.

Another common cause is polycystic ovary syndrome (PCOS) which affects about 10% of women with cycles. Aside from irregular periods, other symptoms might include fluid-filled sacs developing on the ovaries which prevent pregnancy, a hormonal imbalance of androgen which can cause facial hair to grow on girls and increased acne. As you can see, these symptoms are fairly serious but often PCOS goes undetected if a young woman is not tracking her cycle!

Although PCOS can't be cured, it can be managed and treated through good nutrition and medication. Again, since putting on weight affects your hormone levels, maintaining a healthy weight can manage the symptoms of PCOS.

Endometriosis

If your periods are exceptionally <u>painful</u> with <u>heavy bleeding</u>, <u>pelvic pain</u>, or if you have <u>pain with bowel movements</u>, ask to be examined for signs of endometriosis. Endometriosis is <u>a disease in which bits of endometrium, the lining of the uterus, begin to grow outside of the uterus upon the ovaries or other organs of the body</u>. When you have your cycle, this endometrium thickens, breaks down, and bleeds just like the lining inside your uterus, but it is trapped with no way to exit the body. So your body "bandages" it with scar tissue, and this can cause you increasing pain with every cycle.

These scar tissues can eventually prevent a woman from becoming pregnant. Surgery is needed to diagnose endometriosis, but it's always best to catch it early since most endometriosis only becomes worse over time.

There is much to be discovered regarding the cause of endometriosis, but here are some things that can help:

- Take <u>Vitamin D</u>. Most women who contract endometriosis are low in Vitamin D.
- Eat <u>food rich in Omega 3s</u> has been shown to prevent endometriosis.
- Eliminate <u>dairy</u> and <u>gluten</u> from your diet.

General Health

Again, God made you and designed you and gave you yourself, your body and your cycle as a gift to take care of. So it is important that you care for yourself. This might mean searching for a good healthcare professional—a doctor, nurse, midwife, or other specialist—who <u>will listen to you</u> and help you take care of yourself.

Never settle for a healthcare professional who does not listen!

Patients, including young women, have the right of autonomy regarding their health care, which means they are free to listen or not listen to a health care professional's advice. They are free to get a second opinion if they don't trust the professional's advice or if all their questions were not answered.

It's very important to remember that if something is going wrong with your cycle, it is not because you are "broken" or there is something wrong with God's design. It simply means that your body needs extra support and nourishment. Your Father God's design is perfect and if it's not working the way it should, we shouldn't beat our body into submission, but care for it and support it so it can function the way it should. The body's processes should be respected, nourished, and encouraged.

Some professionals sadly do not see a woman's body that way. They see the cycle as a disruption, and fertility as a disease to be cured. They might offer treatments such as artificial hormones as a sort of "band aid" that does not address the root causes. Women have the right to ask their providers to address the underlying causes of their symptoms. Many Catholic healthcare providers are using new treatments such as Natural Procreative (NaPro) technology that address underlying causes and support a woman's natural processes which can actually do much more than just provide a "band aid"!

Remember if you are not comfortable with the care you are receiving ALWAYS get a <u>second</u> <u>opinion</u>!

Understanding the Phases of Your Cycle

Use this chart as an answer key to help your daughter fill in the blank chart in her book on page 54.

	FOLLICULAR PHASE	OVULATION	LUTEAL PHASE	MENSTRUATION
ESTE + PROGE				
DAYS	3-5	5-7	12-14	3-5
FEELINGS				
EAT	• pumpkin or flax seeds • oats • carrots • avocados • cashews • chicken	• corn • tomatoes • almonds • dark chocolate • strawberries • salmon	• sunflower/sesame seeds • brown rice • celery/sweet potatoes • dark chocolate • cucumbers • apples/bananas • beef/turkey • peppermint	• proteins • kale • blueberries • decaf coffee
EXERCISE	• Try some cardio! Run, take a bike ride, hike, organize a game of tag, soccer, or frisbee with friends. • Build your endurance: do your exercises for longer, include extra repetitions, run or walk further distances. • Try weightlifting. Now is the best season to build muscle.	• If you're an athlete, this is your peak training time! • Learn a new skill, perfect a current skill.	• Move to lower intensity cardio: from running to walking or swimming. • Do light strength training. • Try pilates or other exercises that can ease cramps and strengthen your core. • Build endurance.	• Do stretches • Try light cardiovascular exercise like running, jumping jacks, dancing • Work on your core: planks, squats, leg lifts • Rest and recover.

PSALM 139:13-15

My bones are not
hidden from You,
When I was being made
in secret, fashioned in
the depths of the earth.

Your eyes saw me
unformed; in Your book
all are written down;
my days were shaped,
before one came to be.

How precious to me are
Your designs, O God; how
vast the sum of them!

Were I to count them, they
would outnumber the sands;
when I complete them,
still You are with me

Mom, get ready to share your story!

In her book, your daughter will be coming to you to ask for food ideas, so think of some that you would like to share with her. It's fun to make the conversation interesting by maybe sharing a food mishap, like when you added salt instead of sugar to a pie, or dipped cookies into baking powder instead of powdered sugar! All of us have our disaster cooking stories (or maybe it's just me...?).

Another great conversation is to share examples of new foods that you tried and loved, or foods that you tried and will never have again! Sharing these experiences shows her that it's ok to risk and try new things and that it doesn't mean it will always turn out the way you think!

Although the menstruation difficulties mentioned in this session may not happen to you or your daughter ever (I hope they don't!) It's good to have this information in case issues do arise. Especially if you have had issues in the past, it is good for your daughter to know this, since often medical history is an indicator of potential problems. You can make your daughter more aware of what to look for, so problems can be addressed more quickly.

We don't want to cause any young girl additional worry, so if your daughter tends to be anxious, take this time to assure her that with good care and nutrition, chances are high that everything will be fine. And the most important message is that you will be there for her, no matter what!

Here are the questions from her book for you:

- What was your worst cooking disaster?
- What is a food that you hated when you were my age that you actually like now?
- Since you started your cycle, are there any problems that you had? How did you deal with them?
- Make a list of new foods or recipes that you would like to try!

Celebrating Womanhood!

"In the light of Mary, the Church sees in the face of women the reflection of a beauty which mirrors the loftiest sentiments of which the human heart is capable: the self-offering totality of love; the strength that is capable of bearing the greatest sorrows; limitless fidelity and tireless devotion to work; the ability to combine penetrating intuition with words of support and encouragement."

JOHN PAUL II, *REDEMPTORIS MATER*

Beauty and Fashion

Our clothes reveal what we think about <u>ourselves</u>—as people and as a culture. That's why styles change, because ideas change! As Catholics, we need to make sure that we are not being shaped by the secular ideas around us, but that we are continually "transformed by the renewal of our minds" and that includes our clothing choices.

Remember the world's ideas that our bodies don't matter? Are we affected by that? Modernist culture says, "My body is for me." A sacramental Catholic view is that our body is for others. This includes respecting others by our dress. We show this when we wear black at funerals, professional clothes in the workplace or at school, and put on our Sunday best for God.

> "Only the body is capable of making visible what is invisible: the spiritual and the divine."
>
> **ST. JOHN PAUL FEB 20, 1980**

One thing that we are not going to do in this session is give modesty "rules." That is the job of your mom and dad! Cultures differ throughout the world on standards for modesty, as do the values of each family. What we do want is to encourage you to do is discuss your dress with <u>your mom</u> and allow her to help you make good choices

But we will talk about three reasons to care about what you wear.

HOW YOU DRESS MANIFESTS YOUR SOUL

John Paul II explained that our bodies manifest our soul. If that is the case, then what we clothe our bodies with participates in that manifestation. Our clothing should emphasize our personhood, and in women especially, our love of being a <u>woman</u>! Sometimes women think that to be "modest" means we need to hide our feminine form. Think of statues of the Blessed Mother and what she is wearing. Do they emphasize her womanly form? Yes! Because she is a woman, her dress communicates this. Clothing that is used to "<u>hide</u>" our bodies does not communicate truth. What we wear should be an expression of what we <u>believe</u> about <u>ourselves</u>.

HOW YOU DRESS COMMUNICATES YOURSELF TO OTHERS

What you wear should show that you love being a woman, but did you realize that your clothing can actually communicate to others even more about you? <u>Communication</u> happens in all kinds of ways. You can learn a lot about a person without them saying a word. Think about how people communicate by smiling, crying, laughing, or winking. What do we learn about what is going on inside a person by observing them from the outside?

Now consider clothing. A woman who has a dramatic style may communicate that she is confident and not afraid of being noticed. Someone with a more "romantic" style shows her soft nuturing side. A woman with a sporty, natural style communicates strength and openness to adventure. Unique and unusual styles can express a woman's creativity. Professional, classic clothing can communicate a timeless beauty, conservative nature, and leadership ability. None of this encompasses ALL that a woman is or can be, but we need to recognize that style is just one tool for communication between people.

It's good for you to think about your personality and how your style communicates that. As you grow, you learn more about yourself and how you are uniquely made. You will also grow in your personal style and learn how to best communicate who you are by your dress. This is a fun part of growing up!

HOW YOU DRESS IS A FORM OF POSITIVE "SELF-TALK"

Sometimes when we feel down, we need to change our thoughts in order to change our feelings—like we talked about in Session 2. Just as our dress communicates to others, we can also use our dress to communicate to <u>ourselves</u>! Wearing something that we love reminds us that we are wonderfully made— that we are beautiful and wanted. It expresses to ourselves who our Heavenly Father has made us to be.

Sometimes when we are restless and know we need to relax, we can put on clothes that help us feel cozy and comfy. If you are ready for adventure, you may want to get on some sneakers and workout clothes to get moving. If you are feeling good about yourself, you may want to break out your pretty, more dressy outfits that you wouldn't normally wear. Dressing our bodies helps us remind ourselves who we are made to be.

In business, one common tip is "Dress for the job you want to have." That's a good tip in your personal life: dress like the sort of person you want to become. If you want others to respect you and listen to what you have to say, communicate that in your clothing. If you want others to find you friendly and approachable, you can communicate this through your clothing, too.

Resources for you!

The Five Style Personalities

(https://stylecoachinginstitute.com/mini-personal-styling-masterclass-style-personalities/)

Here are five different ways of expressing yourself through clothes. We feel most confident when our clothing reflects who we are, not an image of what we admire in others. Check out these five "style personalities" and see if one of them resonates with you!

CREATIVE

- Fun, creative pieces that mix and match
- Jewelry is bold and modern
- Eye-catching statement accessories
- Strong bright colors
- Different than everyone else
- People never know what you will wear
- Unusual lines and shapes
- Lots of different types of clothes
- Makeup is experimental and new
- Finds styles at thrift stores, bohemian, modern, boutiques

DRAMATIC

- Striking colors and large prints
- Priority is the "wow" factor
- Clothing is not necessarily practical, but stylish
- Dramatic makeup
- Tends to be overdressed than underdressed
- Doesn't mind attracting the attention of others
- Metallic, animal prints or shiny material
- Bold, well-styled and confident
- Finds styles at Forever 21, Urban Outfitters, Anthropologie

NATURAL

- Comfort is key
- Easy to wear and not "fussy"
- Simple lines and basic colors
- Jewelry includes wood, shell, stones, natural materials
- Doesn't like being over-dressed
- Minimal to no makeup
- Accessories are few and understated
- Anything eye-catching is just a detail, not a main piece
- Tend to neutrals and natural fabrics like brown leather, linen, and cotton
- Finds styles at Old Navy, Lands End, American Eagle, Express, Aeropostale

ROMANTIC

- Feminine, pretty colors like pastels
- Details include ruffles, lace, and appliques
- Material tends to be full and drapey
- Soft lines with bust or waist definition
- Patterns are subtle, floral, and understated
- Likes to wear perfume and subtle makeup
- Prefers skirts and dresses to pants
- Finds styles at Petal Lush, Vera Wang, Baltic Born, April Cornell

CLASSIC

- Timeless look
- Quality over quantity
- Smart, understated, designed to not attract attention
- Soft folds and straight lines
- Tailored and not baggy or loose
- Prefers pants to jeans or sweats
- Colors all match in classic combinations
- Classic shoe styles
- Makeup is safe and predictable
- Find styles at Ann Taylor, Nordstrom, White House Black Market

Check out some of these Catholic women and what they are doing to provide tools and ideas for communicating truth by how we dress!

- LillianFallon.com
- NicoleMCaruso.com
- LitanyNYC.com
- MeghanAshleyStyling.com
- TelosArtShop.com
- Siena-Co.com Swimwear
- Catholic Dress Co.

"Progress usually tends to be measured according to the criteria of science and technology...Much more important is the social and ethical dimension, which deals with human relations and spiritual values. In this area... society certainly owes much to the "genius of women"."

ST. JOHN PAUL
LETTER TO WOMEN

Moms, a great way to give your daughter fashion inspiration is to subscribe to catalogs of quality clothing that fit your family's modesty rules and your daughter's budding style. Look at the catalogs together and talk about styles. Many catalogs are free and can provide inspiration for putting together outfits or even ideas for surprise gifts.

The brands above are included just for reference: they in no way imply an endorsement of their philosophies or products. But often you can find independent or smaller companies you want to support by googling "style like Old Navy," etc.

You Are Not Alone

Community of Women

When Christ was born, He came into a world that largely did not value women. Women in ancient cultures were often seen as second-class citizens or merely property of men. Jesus made it clear that God does not see His masterpiece, woman, as any less than man. As a man, Jesus treated women with dignity, spoke to them about His truth, and chose them as His first witnesses to mankind. Our Lady was the first to know about Christ! And the first woman to proclaim the Resurrection was a woman, St. Mary Magdalene.

Baptism made men and women equal in the Church, and Christian women took that equality seriously. Christian women began to educate other women, care for the poor, sick, and handicapped, and changed the way people thought about medicine: as something that everyone deserved, not just those with money. Women saved babies from infanticide, rescued people from abuse, and helped build Christian culture. The Church today informs all people that women are equal in dignity and that their gifts and call are necessary to the world.

Sadly, not all women have experienced this truth. There have been times in history when women could not vote or own property. Even today, there are many places where women are oppressed and not given the same opportunities as men. Attitudes towards women vary between cultures, time periods, and countries.

But, no matter what the laws or cultures dictate, God tells us that each woman always is worthy of dignity, for she brings to the world unique gifts and insights. Women are equal to men in dignity before God, even though our gifts are very different.

Don't be fooled by those who say that in order to have worth, you need to act like a boy, or like a man. The gifts that women bring to the world are worthy of acknowledgement! The world historically has not valued women's contributions in science, art, and literature, and women have not always been given the same credit as men for their work. Yet their importance should not be ignored. Those women who have gone before us have paved the way for us—not by being like men, but by bringing their feminine insights to the world.

And don't forget the saints! There are so many women in Heaven who are rooting for us and praying for us, especially Our Lady. Learn their stories, talk to them, and ask for their prayers. This is a community of women that reaches beyond death into eternity.

THE IMPORTANCE OF FRIENDSHIPS

Never forget that you need other women. Friendships are a gift from God, but they need to be developed, nurtured, and encouraged just like any relationship. It can be hard to learn how to get along with other girls, especially when you are young and still learning how to handle hurt feelings or settle differences of opinion. Remember to be patient with others and as hard as it may be, assume the best. Don't automatically think that others are being mean or ignoring you. Instead, try to understand where they are coming from first and think the best about them.

> May the words of my mouth and the meditation of my heart be pleasing in Your sight, O Lord, my Rock and my Redeemer.
>
> **PSALM 19:14**

One thing that really destroys friendships is gossip. Gossip is when you talk about other people behind their back. This hurts people more than anything else you can do! If you say something that is mean or untrue about another person, you can never take it back, because you because you have given others an impression of that person that they will remember and pass on to others. And this is before social media gets involved!

The ancient Greeks had a saying that the words you speak should pass through three gates, or tests.

- Is it true?
- Is it necessary?
- Is it kind?

The world often tries to pit women against one another. In movies and shows, women are shown to be always competing for attention or for a boyfriend. But Christ changed all this. He reminds women that what is important about us is not our youth, talents, or attractiveness but the fact that we are precious in His sight. When we put Him first, He can build a genuine sisterhood among us that is not based on competition but on Him.

YOUR FAMILY

The most important women in your life should be those in your family. Why? Because you were not created as a disconnected, solitary island. You came from a long line of women who gave birth, fed, taught, and nurtured their daughters who then did the same for their own daughters, over and over again till it got to you! Every woman came from a woman!

The family that God has given you are the people who will always be with you. Most of your friends will come and go through the years, but your family stays the same. There is something very special about that. Think about your mother, aunts, grandmother, sisters, cousins, and the other women in your family. They have been through the same experiences of growing up that you are going through, and this has given them insight and wisdom.

It's good to take time to talk to the older women in your life and learn their stories. Many women have histories that you may not know about until you ask! There are many inspiring women in history, but the best inspiration is from the women that you come from. Even if you don't know them well, their stories are worth knowing. **Your daughter can use pages 65-68 to interview two living relatives and learning about two relatives who have already died.**

Conclusion

Our challenge as Catholic women is to build a true community of women between the generations, so that a culture of life which values a woman's gifts can be built up in the world. Never forget how much you are loved and cherished by your Heavenly Father Who has made you perfectly and wonderfully.

Thank you for taking this course! If it has been helpful to you, please let us know by contacting us through messyfamilyproject.org.

PSALM 139

O Lord, You have searched
me and known me.
You know when I sit down
and when I rise up;
  You discern my thoughts from far away.
You search out my path and my lying down
  and are acquainted with all my ways.
Even before a word is on my tongue,
  O Lord, You know it completely.
You hem me in, behind and before,
  and lay Your hand upon me.
Such knowledge is too wonderful for me;
  it is so high that I cannot attain it.

Where can I go from Your spirit?
  Or where can I flee from Your presence?
If I ascend to heaven, You are there;
  if I make my bed in Sheol, You are there.
If I take the wings of the morning
  and settle at the farthest limits of the sea,
even there Your hand shall lead me,
  and Your right hand shall hold me fast.
If I say, "Surely the darkness shall cover me,
  and night wraps itself around me,"
even the darkness is not dark to You;
  the night is as bright as the day,
  for darkness is as light to You.

For it was You who formed my inward parts;
  You knit me together in my mother's womb.
I praise You, for I am fearfully
and wonderfully made.

Wonderful are Your works;
that I know very well.
  My frame was not hidden from You,
when I was being made in secret,
  intricately woven in the
depths of the earth.
Your eyes beheld my unformed substance.
In Your book were written
  all the days that were formed for me,
  when none of them as yet existed.
How weighty to me are Your thoughts, O God!
  How vast is the sum of them!
I try to count them—they are
more than the sand;
  I come to the end—I am still with You.

O that You would kill the wicked, O God,
  and that the bloodthirsty
would depart from me—
those who speak of You maliciously
  and lift themselves up against You for evil!
Do I not hate those who hate You, O Lord?
  And do I not loathe those
who rise up against You?
I hate them with perfect hatred;
  I count them my enemies.
Search me, O God, and know my heart;
  test me and know my thoughts.
See if there is any wicked way in me,
  and lead me in the way everlasting.